AN IDEAS INTO ACTION GUIDEBOOK

Managing
Ambition

Ideas Into Action Guidebooks

Aimed at managers and executives who are concerned with their own and others' development, each guidebook in this series gives specific advice on how to complete a developmental task or solve a leadership problem.

CONTRIBUTORS	Anand Chandrasekar, Craig Chappelow, Kim Leahy, Lynn Miller, Doug Riddle, Bertrand Sereno
DIRECTOR OF ASSESSMENTS, TOOLS, AND PUBLICATIONS	Sylvester Taylor
MANAGER, PUBLICATION DEVELOPMENT	Peter Scisco
EDITORS	Stephen Rush Karen Lewis
ASSOCIATE EDITOR	Shaun Martin
WRITER	Martin Wilcox
DESIGN AND LAYOUT	Joanne Ferguson
COVER DESIGN	Laura J. Gibson Chris Wilson, 29 & Company

CCL No. 453
ISBN No. 978-1-60491-148-0

CENTER FOR CREATIVE LEADERSHIP
POST OFFICE BOX 26300
GREENSBORO, NORTH CAROLINA 27438-6300
336-288-7210
WWW.CCL.ORG / PUBLICATIONS

AN IDEAS INTO ACTION GUIDEBOOK

Managing Ambition

Center for
Creative
Leadership

www.ccl.org

THE IDEAS INTO ACTION GUIDEBOOK SERIES

This series of guidebooks draws on the practical knowledge that the Center for Creative Leadership (CCL) has generated since its inception in 1970. The purpose of the series is to provide leaders with specific advice on how to complete a developmental task or solve a leadership challenge. In doing that, the series carries out CCL's mission to advance the understanding, practice, and development of leadership for the benefit of society worldwide.

CCL's unique position as a research and education organization supports a community of accomplished scholars and educators in a community of shared knowledge. CCL's knowledge community holds certain principles in common, and its members work together to understand and generate practical responses to the ever-changing circumstances of leadership and organizational challenges.

In its interactions with a richly varied client population, in its research into the effect of leadership on organizational performance and sustainability, and in its deep insight into the workings of organizations, CCL creates new, sound ideas that leaders all over the world put into action every day. We believe you will find the Ideas Into Action Guidebooks an important addition to your leadership toolkit.

Table of Contents

In Brief

Ambition is a good thing, but too much of it can cause problems. You need ambition to be successful, but if you have too much, it can derail your career. This guidebook will help you determine whether you have a problem with ambition. You will gain a fuller understanding of its basic drivers: the need for competence, the need for achievement, and the need for rewards. You will learn how these drivers can affect your work, and you will learn strategies for managing them.

Each of the drivers has identifiable components. The need for competence, for example, has three components: superiority, competitiveness, and pride. The exercises in this guidebook will help you identify which components could be a problem for you and prioritize your efforts in addressing them. You will also be encouraged to seek ongoing feedback from others and to observe and learn from how other leaders deal with their ambition.

With this guidebook, you can learn to understand and manage your ambition so that it won't derail your career but will contribute to your efforts to achieve personal and organizational success.

The Paradox of Ambition

If you're a manager, you're probably ambitious. You want to be right, achieve great things, and be rewarded and recognized for what you've done. That's good. Without ambition, it's unlikely that you would have taken on management responsibilities, which most leaders acknowledge as very challenging. Furthermore, ambition can drive success—for you and for your organization.

But CCL research shows that leaders who don't handle their ambition properly can damage their careers and undercut their efforts to advance their organizations. That is the paradox of ambition: While it is a necessary factor in business success, too much of it can derail a career.

This guidebook will help you understand and manage your ambition so that it won't derail your career but will contribute to your efforts to achieve personal and organizational success.

When a Strength Becomes a Weakness

CCL has conducted extensive studies on executive success and derailment. This research

7

consistently reports that leaders cite ambition as a reason for career success. Many executives rely on ambition to drive their work. However, the very same ambition that drives executives to the top can have serious consequences if they do not keep it in check.

When leaders become overly ambitious, they are often arrogant. They promote themselves, without the performance to support their claims and beyond their level of competence. They are overconfident, presenting themselves as capable of more than they actually are, and highly political, using manipulation to gain promotions. They are focused primarily on themselves, they manage up without paying much attention to peers or direct reports, and they are willing to step on people to move up. In short, the strength of ambition becomes a weakness.

Problems leaders encounter due to excessive ambition:

- Poor follow-through and poor strategic decisions—the leader's success criteria are focused on self and not on the organization.
- Poor interpersonal relationships—others view the leader as too focused on self-interests.
- Lack of trust—others see overly ambitious leaders taking credit beyond their due.

In CCL's research, the executives who derailed were not unaccomplished. They had achieved high-level positions, but they failed to manage their ambition. This didn't have to happen. It's possible to be ambitious and not to derail.

The problem of too much ambition can vary from one organization to the next. In some organizations it's nearly impossible to be overly ambitious. For example, a fast-moving company that

Assessing the correct level of ambition for your organization or situation can be tricky. Younger or newer members of an organization may show excessive ambition as a means of proving themselves to their new superiors, and older employees may temper their ambition for the good of the organization. Research shows that both these approaches can lead to problems. CCL has found that moderate levels of ambition can be the most successful in advancing your goals and your career. However, CCL also recommends flexibility in your level of ambition. Some situations (such as finishing an important project or working toward a promotion) may require you to increase your ambition in order to be successful, while others (like leading a new team or department with established protocols and techniques) require less ambition and assertiveness in order to benefit the team. In other words, moderation in ambition is often the best solution, but keep your eyes open and remain flexible when the situation calls for it.

rewards aggressive behavior may have a higher tolerance for overly ambitious individuals than a firm with traditional views of career advancement. In spite of these differences, CCL's research indicates that ambition that gets in the way of performance will lead to derailment in most organizations.

So you must first determine whether you have a problem. How ambitious are you? Could your ambition lead you to a crisis? Use Exercise 1 to make a quick assessment.

Exercise 1: Measure Your Ambition

In this exercise, consider your current level of ambition in four different categories, and use the illustration to help discover any areas where your ambition may be holding you back.

For each category, rate yourself on a scale from 1 to 5, with 1 being a moderate level of ambition and 5 being an extremely high level of ambition. Use the sample statements in the table as a guide. Then fill in the corresponding sections in the circle. For example, if you rate yourself 4 on recognition, then fill in sections 1–4 in that section.

Category	Moderate (1)	Extreme (5)
Recognition	I seek to be recognized by my superiors and my direct reports.	I often tout my accomplishments to my superiors and direct reports as a way of raising my reputation.
Work Ethic	I am a hard worker, but I know when to slow down.	I will stop at nothing and sacrifice anything in order to achieve my goals.
Competitiveness	I am competitive with other members of my organization, but I come together with others for the good of the company.	My competitiveness has caused conflicts between other groups and departments, as well as rivalries between my colleagues.
Individual Success	I am satisfied with my contributions to the goals of the company, and I put its goals ahead of my desire to be right.	I always want to be right, even if it is counterproductive to the organization's goals.

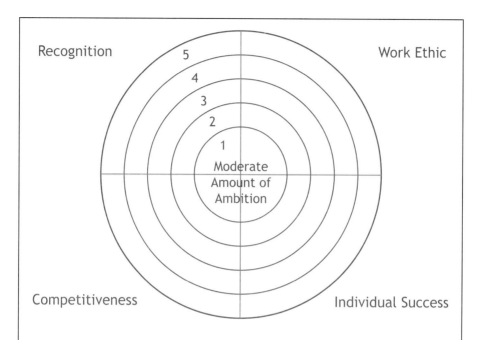

When you've rated yourself on all the categories and filled in your circle, take a look at it. Any sections that are 3 or above may signal that you need to address your ambition in that area. Also, pay attention if the filled-in area of your circle is somewhat lopsided—this could signal that you need to tone down one or more particular areas.

Note: This assessment does not seek to provide a precise measurement of your ambition; rather, it should be viewed as a rough estimate and as a guide for future development.

If Exercise 1 suggests that you may have a problem, it's important that you gain a more detailed understanding of ambition, especially its basic drivers and their components. Along with that, seek out other sources of information, such as feedback from coworkers. Also very useful in this regard would be a careful examination of any formal 360-degree assessments in which you have recently participated. (CCL designs these assessments to gather feedback from peers, bosses, and direct reports.)

Let's look at the drivers of ambition.

The Drivers of Ambition

CCL research identifies three basic drivers of ambition:

- **The need for competence.** You want to appear competent and be competent. You want to always make the right decisions and do the right things. You are intensely driven by the need to get it right the first time, every time.

- **The need for achievement.** You work hard and want to appear to work hard. You drive yourself and others with intense pressure to perform.

- **The need for rewards.** You want to be successful and to feel and be seen as successful. You want the perks, privileges, and honors that accompany success.

These drivers have identifiable components, each of which you should assess and manage. The following sections in this guidebook will help you do just that.

The Need for Competence

The need for competence has three components: superiority, competitiveness, and pride. It is important for you to be an expert in what you do, to win, and to be confident in your capabilities. More than anything, what distinguishes leaders driven by their need for competence is the desire to get it right—each and every time. They want to be experts in whatever jobs they tackle. These components can play out as extreme and overly ambitious, or moderate and appropriately ambitious.

Superiority

When you take superiority to its extreme, you take satisfaction from feeling morally and intellectually better than others. It's extremely important that others see you and you see yourself as first or right, rather than liked—even if it is counterproductive to organizational goals.

In its moderate form, you take satisfaction in your contribution to the achievement of organizational goals, and you modify your personal desire to be right. You focus—from an organizational and task perspective—on achieving business results, producing desired outcomes, and reaching team goals.

Competitiveness

When you take competitiveness to its extreme, you compete to the point that you are involved frequently in both individual rivalries and conflicts between departments or groups. You tend to categorize others as either on your side or wrong.

In its moderate form, you have your own strong opinions about people and ideas, but you work hard not to always see things as black or white. When you do, you work to let your initial reactions subside and to see the shades of gray—the good and bad in both yourself and others.

Pride

When you take pride to its extreme, you believe that the organization could not run as well as it does if you weren't there. You are constantly conscious of your own agenda, which always involves making sure you look good to the people who matter. You value your own way of doing things over all others, believing you are uniquely qualified to know what is best.

In its moderate form, you have a strong sense of self-confidence and enjoy reaping the rewards of your efforts, but you work to make realistic claims of how good or important your own skills are to the job at hand. You recognize that your value to the organization will enhance your opportunities for individual advancement. You have confidence in your own convictions, but you also see others' perspectives.

Let's look at an example of how leaders with an extremely strong need for competence might let the elements of superiority, competitiveness, and pride affect their work.

Jim has been named to lead a project task force assigned to decrease the production cycle dramatically for his company's flagship product. Early in team meetings, two clear choices emerge: Jim's idea of a major investment in new technology and Craig's idea of making slight changes to the current assembly line that will streamline the process. Jim might be tempted to react in the following ways:

- Identify Craig as a rival or the enemy—not just as a person with another point of view.

- Mobilize to win the fight.

- Process and present information that confirms why he is right, disregard Craig's point of view, and hide information that supports it.

- Hold and express the belief that Craig's approach is incomplete, weak, or morally objectionable.

- Feign a democratic approach to leading the team through the process but pursue a hidden agenda to achieve his own goal.

- Cite examples of his past successes as grounds for pursuing his current idea.

- Keep track of who sides with whom, and judge people accordingly.

Jim's not being able to manage his extremely strong need for competence could result in the team's not sharing information. It could create a division within the task force, lead people to believe that Jim is self-serving, and prevent the task force from reaching its goal.

Using Exercise 2, examine your own behavior to determine whether your need for competence may be causing you to be overly ambitious.

Exercise 2: The Need for Competence

Let's look at three areas to determine your own need for competence: feedback, relationships, and self. Use this checklist to mark the categories that best apply to you.

Category	Behavior	Check
Feedback	Others often refer to me as a perfectionist.	
	Others often refer to me as overly competitive or driven to win.	
	Others refer to me as overly assertive and demanding in my requests.	
Relationships	I have been driven by a need to be right, and that drive has impacted my relationships with others.	
	I am or have been involved in highly competitive rivalries with other individuals or groups.	
	I prioritize being right over fostering developmental working relationships with colleagues and direct reports.	
Self	I have a great deal of pride in my work.	
	I have trouble listening to others' opinions or integrating them into my personal viewpoint and decisions.	
	I sometimes place work demands ahead of my own needs and those of my family.	

Now think about the areas where you display the most negative ambitious traits. What are some steps you can take to improve in these areas? For instance, if you're often receiving feedback that others perceive you as overly ambitious, think about your behaviors that could contribute to that perception and how to alter them.

How the Need for Competence Affects Your Work for the Organization

Overly ambitious managers may dismiss concerns about their own behavior, believing that moderating their behavior is a sign of weakness. However, keep in mind that your behavior influences the way that others perceive you. It can ultimately affect your ability to get things done for your organization, not to mention your career advancement.

Strategies for Managing Ambition Driven by Competence

If you believe you are powerfully motivated by the need to be right or to win, and you are concerned about being seen as overly ambitious, consider the following strategies for managing that need:

- If you are experiencing conflict, openly acknowledge the conflict and direct yourself and others through the process of finding the best solution.

- Seek first to understand alternative views by listening, ask follow-up questions, and make validating statements of other people's comments.

- Seek to show respect for opposing views by incorporating as much as possible of those views in your own ideas.

- Don't keep track of whose view is being adopted or who is winning, but instead judge outcomes based on how they advance organizational goals.

- Don't worry about whether you are seen as right or winning; focus on understanding the fairness and value of the process.

- Clearly state and discuss your concerns about your own view and opposing views, and give each a fair shake in the process.

- Feature and highlight the positive contributions of oᴜ.
  as well as your own.

The Need for Achievement

The need for achievement has three components: drive, control, and power. Your work is important to you, and it is important for you to get things done your way and to have authority over others. What distinguishes leaders who are driven by their need for achievement is their desire to be in charge and a strong, internalized ethic of hard work—from themselves and others. They push themselves and their team. They create an intense, sometimes exhausting environment. As with the components of competitiveness, these components can play out as extreme and overly ambitious, or moderate and appropriately ambitious.

Drive

When you take drive to its extreme, you push yourself to the limit. You are so totally absorbed in your work that it sometimes acts as a near addiction and you do not know what to do with your time when you are not working. In the process, you often push others to produce results without acknowledging organizational and situational factors.

In its moderate form, you are exceptionally hardworking, bursting with the energy to accomplish a long list of tasks, but you have trained yourself to set priorities and moderate your behavior. You ease up when you receive feedback that it is time to slow down. You expect others to work hard but remain aware of the practical limits that affect their performance.

Control

When you take control to its extreme, you prefer to behave unilaterally, believing you know what is best for what needs to be done. You often resist following other people's agendas, you have a strong belief in your ability to take over and fix things, and you often behave in ways that are seen as abrasive because you do not have time for input from others.

In its moderate form, you are an effective problem solver. You enjoy taking charge when necessary and work hard to stop short of a complete takeover of problem situations. You consciously try to remain receptive to the influence of your direct reports and their need for autonomy.

Power

When power is taken to its extreme, you actively seek, acquire, and maintain power. You work hard at making sure no one bypasses your chain of command, and you attempt to be in charge and be seen as in charge.

In its moderate form, you seek, acquire, and maintain power for its use in achieving business results, sharing it when necessary to obtain goals. You accept and enjoy your responsibility, and you work hard at not giving the impression that you are flaunting it.

Using Exercise 3, examine your own behavior to determine whether your need for achievement may be causing you to be overly ambitious.

Let's look at an example of how leaders with an excessively strong need for achievement might let the elements of drive, control, and power affect their work.

Ellen is a few months into a new role leading the effort to move her company into a new international market. She is sitting on a series of past successes and enjoys a reputation as a star performer. Her company is in a period of explosive growth and great change. Ellen might be tempted to react in the following ways:

- See her entire role as an ongoing crisis intervention requiring extraordinary time, energy, and focus.

- Believe that, to lead her team, she must be the first one in and the last one out.

- Achieve results, push and keep pushing—both herself and others.

- Take control quickly when a meeting or process bogs down, jettisoning agreed-upon procedures and substituting her own.

- Delegate responsibility without authority, preferring to keep her hold on the information and resources necessary to work the problem herself.

- Push her own agenda relentlessly, not stopping to hear the views of others and sometimes exploiting others in service of her own goals.

Ellen's not being able to manage her excessively strong need for achievement could result in her not sharing information, fatigue for herself and others on her team, and a trail of bruised egos. She could spread herself too thin and miss deadlines. She might only receive compliance from individuals about the new market when she really needs total acceptance. She could potentially damage family and personal relationships.

Exercise 3: The Need for Achievement

The purpose of these questions is to help you gain an understanding of how driven you are by the need for achievement, how it might manifest itself in overly ambitious behavior, and how that drive might impact others. Use this assessment to develop a picture of how your need for achievement may be harming your professional development.

What are the actual hours you work? How do your hours compare to those of your peers?

When you are pushing toward a goal, do you ever say no to a new project or task? If not, what keeps you from saying no?

In the past few years, what personal activities have you declined because of your workload?

If you asked your close friends and family members whether you do too much, what would be their answer?

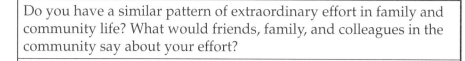

Do you have a similar pattern of extraordinary effort in family and community life? What would friends, family, and colleagues in the community say about your effort?

Now review your answers. Is there a pattern of overambitious behavior? If so, how is your need for achievement contributing to the problem?

How the Need for Achievement Affects Your Work for the Organization

It can be particularly difficult to gain self-awareness in this area. When the need for achievement drives behavior, managers may see only the positive effects. The manager may believe, "I am working so hard and sacrificing so much—how can that be overly ambitious?"

Any managerial behavior, even one tied to achievement, can have negative effects if you carry it to an extreme. To judge whether your behavior has moved into negative territory, first recognize that you are in fact being driven by the need for achievement. The second step is to consider its impact on yourself and others. By doing this, you will be able to distinguish for yourself the negative impact it has on your performance and career.

Strategies for Managing Ambition Driven by Achievement

If you believe you are powerfully motivated by the need to be in charge, and you are concerned about being seen as overly ambitious, consider the following strategies for managing that need:

- Accept the challenge of your role, but view it as a task, not a crisis.

- Lead by example, but do what can be done within your limits and trust that others will do the same.

- Learn to decline projects and responsibilities when you are already overloaded with work. To help prioritize your responsibilities, ask yourself the following question: Will taking on this work help or hinder my career, my personal life, my family life, and my involvement with my community? If you are consistently helping your career at the expense of the other three, you will quickly learn the value of taking on certain projects and excluding others.

- Expect results from yourself and others, but also listen and watch for signs that you or others are approaching the limits of performance.

- Work to be patient with processes, allowing them to play out without taking over and assuming all responsibility.

Declining or saying no to a project at work may be easy and acceptable in some cultures, but in others, saying no is considered extremely rude. For instance, in Indonesia, it is considered impolite to disagree with someone or to say no to a request. Indonesians will instead often suck air through their teeth as a means of saying no, rather than stating it directly. In Japan, people often avoid saying no directly. They may instead say they will think about it or even say yes out of politeness, even though they may actually mean no. As with any other aspect of dealing with a new culture, one must be aware of local customs and traditions in order to communicate effectively.

- Delegate responsibility and authority, allowing others the autonomy to create their own successes.
- Take the time to stop and moderate effort based on the shared goals of your entire group and organization.
- Learn to do other things outside of work.
- Plan to celebrate successes, and pause to point toward new goals.
- Seek feedback from friends and family about how much time they think they should be getting from you, and work to plan that time as part of your schedule.

The Need for Rewards

The need for rewards has three components: recognition, profile, and status. It is important to have others acknowledge your work, to maintain a positive image, and to have an important role in an organization. More than anything, what distinguishes leaders driven by their need for rewards is the desire to receive recognition for their competence and achievement, sometimes even a kind of heroic status. As with the components for competence and achievement, these factors can play out as extreme and overly ambitious, or moderate and appropriately ambitious.

Recognition

When you take recognition to its extreme, it's very important to you to be acknowledged for the work that you do. You often put yourself in high-profile situations to ensure that you will be recognized, and in doing so, you strive to make sure other people are aware of your good work. You don't see yourself as showing off; you are just making sure people know of your accomplishments.

In its moderate form, you want to be well known and well liked, and you feel good when that happens. You also remind yourself of the underlying accomplishments that brought you that recognition and consistently strive to have the work speak for itself.

Profile

When you take your concern for profile to its extreme, your image is very important to you and you work hard to maintain it, sometimes without the accomplishments to back it up. From the clothes you wear to the people you want to be seen with, you carefully orchestrate the message you want others to receive about you.

In its moderate form, you enjoy a high-profile challenge but do the homework and follow-through necessary to earn the acknowledgement associated with the project or job. Your image is important to you, but you want to look good based on your hard work.

Status

When you take the desire for status to its extreme, you are very concerned with levels and chains of command within an organization. It's important to you that others acknowledge and respect your position. You work hard at maintaining your status within the organization, and you immensely enjoy the perks associated with your status.

In its moderate form, you are conscious of your status and work to make sure others do not see you as too directive. You recognize the impact your status can have on the flow of information, and you enjoy the perks of your status and share them with others. You work to engage individuals at all levels within the organization.

Using Exercise 4, examine your own behavior to determine whether your need for rewards may be causing you to be overly ambitious.

24

Let's look at an example of how leaders with an extremely strong need for rewards might let the elements of recognition, profile, and status affect their work.

Sam was recently put in charge of the company's marketing and sales function. He is charged with maintaining a strong but steady growth rate and market share while entering a key new market. Sam might be tempted to react in the following ways:

- Announce his plans to enter the new market personally, publicly, and with great fanfare.

- Take every opportunity to magnify and keep his efforts in the corporate eye, milking others for compliments and congratulation.

- Spend a large part of his time overseeing the creation of public displays of his individual and group progress, in publications, speaking, and electronic media.

- Save for himself opportunities to present to the board of directors and influential groups and individuals.

- Be extremely involved in the project's visible stages but leave the everyday grunt work to others.

- Keep track of and secure the perks of his position for himself: the best office, privileges, and status symbols.

- Speak directly with only certain members of his organization on terms he deems appropriate, and always maintain his status as the leader.

If Sam can't manage his extremely strong need for rewards, it could result in his not sharing information. Individuals below him in the organization may resent and disrespect him. He may never really understand the actual work that is being done and therefore not be able to effectively manage it. There may be a sense of haves and have-nots within the organization.

Exercise 4: The Need for Rewards

Highs and Lows
Think of the last time you felt elated by receiving an external reward, and the last time you felt down when failing to receive recognition.

- What did the high feel like?

- The low?

- How would the middle ground feel different?

Status
Can you remember a time when you kept score of whether you were up or down with respect to symbols of status and public profile?

- Why were these things important to you?

- How did they make you feel?

- What would you lose without having them, or gain by obtaining them?

Limelight
Look back on a time of great satisfaction when you were in the limelight.

- What about the limelight attracted you?

- What did you enjoy about your own reaction? What did you enjoy about the reactions of others?

- Did you sometimes feel idle or unproductive during the downtime between public successes?

- If so, what was missing that impacted your productivity?

How the Need for Rewards Affects Your Work for the Organization

This guidebook isn't suggesting that you not promote yourself. Rather, you should not promote yourself exclusively. As with the other drivers of ambition, the need for rewards is not negative in itself. Without self-awareness, however, it can contribute to excessive ambition and lead to derailment. If you promote yourself solely and excessively, others are likely to resent you. By being willing to share the glory, you often put yourself in a better light with others.

Strategies for Managing Ambition Driven by Rewards

If you believe you are powerfully motivated by the need to receive recognition, and you are concerned about being seen as overly ambitious, consider the following strategies for managing that need:

- Work to delay the gratification that comes with success until you have achieved your goal, instead directing your focus and that of your team on intermediate performance goals.

- Couch your performance and that of your team in the context of organizational goals, not individual and group goals.

- Spread the opportunities to take credit for the work of your group among members of the group, not just for yourself. Make it a conscious part of your schedule.

- Involve yourself in not just the glamorous parts of the work but also the everyday routines that make success possible.

- Keep yourself and your group focused on agreed-upon goals which lead to success, showing by example that the symbols of success do not matter.

- Share the perks and privileges of your role with your team.

Moving Forward

You should now have a good understanding of the drivers of ambition and their components. The next step is for you to identify which of these could be a problem for you and to address them. Use Exercise 5 to prioritize your efforts.

Exercise 5: Assessing and Addressing Your Ambition

1. For each component, circle E or M in the *You* column to indicate whether you consider your behavior extreme or moderate.

2. For each component, circle E or M in the *Others* column to indicate what you estimate to be the consensus of people who have given you feedback about your behavior.

3. For each component, assign a priority. If you have circled E in both columns, circle 1 in the *Priority* column. If you have circled M in the *You* column and E in the *Others* column, circle 2. If you have circled E in the *You* column and M in the *Others* column, circle 3. If you have circled M in both columns, circle 4.

	You	Others	Priority
The Need for Competence			
Superiority	E M	E M	1 2 3 4
Competitiveness	E M	E M	1 2 3 4
Pride	E M	E M	1 2 3 4
The Need for Achievement			
Drive	E M	E M	1 2 3 4
Control	E M	E M	1 2 3 4
Power	E M	E M	1 2 3 4
The Need for Rewards			
Recognition	E M	E M	1 2 3 4
Profile	E M	E M	1 2 3 4
Status	E M	E M	1 2 3 4

The more components you have with 1 or 2, the more your career and ability to promote organizational success may be in jeopardy. You should seek feedback on any component with a 1, 2, or 3, beginning with the highest-priority components.

You can immediately begin to manage your ambition by addressing the high-priority components indicated by Exercise 5 and using the suggestions for moderation given in this guidebook. But you should also take additional action by seeking ongoing feedback on how well you are managing your ambition. To gain feedback that can benefit you the most, consider whom to ask, when to ask, and what kind of feedback you want.

When you think about whom to ask for feedback, think of a person whose opinion you respect and who will encourage you to improve your effectiveness. It's also helpful to ask someone whose work style is different from your own so that you gain access to a new point of view. The person you seek feedback from should be someone you must interact with in order for you both to get results—this gives both of you a vested interest in the feedback process.

In choosing when to ask for feedback, keep in mind that you should have already identified which drivers and components of ambition are your priority. Another consideration is frequency. The more often you receive feedback, the more often you can take positive action to manage your ambition.

Once you decide whom to ask and when, you need to know the form the feedback should take. CCL recommends the Situation-Behavior-Impact model, or SBI. This means of sharing feedback is very effective and simple. The person giving you feedback should describe the situation in which he or she observed you, describe your behavior in that situation, and then tell you what kind of impact your behavior had on him or her.

When you have received the feedback, it will then be your job to evaluate its content: Is it accurate? Will it help you manage your ambition? In addition to seeking ongoing feedback, continue to observe and learn from how other managers deal with their ambition.

Ambition as a Developmental Opportunity

Ambition can be a powerful force, driving your career and helping you leverage the work of others to advance your organization. But if you don't manage it well, ambition can do much more harm than good. It is also intricately related to other managerial strengths that can become weaknesses. That's why you must put ambition into a larger developmental context, where it plays out with other management characteristics such as self-awareness and empathy, and with essential organizational activities such as collaboration, teamwork, and visioning.

To put it into context, engage in a formal process involving a valid and reliable 360-degree evaluation, followed by a carefully conceived and supported development plan. This is an ambitious undertaking, but for many managers—and very likely for you— that's a positive.

Background

The Center for Creative Leadership has long conducted ground-breaking research on derailment, contrasting those people who make it to the top with those who derail. These studies identify characteristics that make the difference between continuing to advance and derailing—that is, leaving the organization involuntarily or reaching a plateau. This research has been subsequently confirmed by data from Benchmarks, CCL's comprehensive 360-degree assessment tool that identifies strengths and development needs, encourages and guides change, and offers strategic insights for middle and upper-middle managers and executives.

Suggested Resources

Browning, H., & Van Velsor, E. (1999). *Three keys to development: Defining and meeting your leadership challenges.* Greensboro, NC: Center for Creative Leadership.

Hernez-Broome, G., McLaughlin, C., & Trovas, S. (2006). *Selling yourself without selling out: A leader's guide to ethical self-promotion.* Greensboro, NC: Center for Creative Leadership.

Kaplan, R. E., Drath, W. H., & Kofodimos, J. R. (1991). *Beyond ambition: How driven managers can lead better and live better.* San Francisco, CA: Jossey-Bass.

King, S. N., & Altman, D. G. (2011). *Discovering the leader in you: Workbook.* San Francisco, CA: Jossey-Bass.

King, S. N., Altman, D. G., & Lee, R. J. (2011). *Discovering the leader in you: How to realize your leadership potential* (2nd ed.). San Francisco, CA: Jossey-Bass.

Kirkland, K., & Manoogian, S. (1998). *Ongoing feedback: How to get it, how to use it.* Greensboro, NC: Center for Creative Leadership.

Leslie, J. B., & Van Velsor, E. (1996). *A look at derailment today: North America and Europe.* Greensboro, NC: Center for Creative Leadership.

Lombardo, M. M., & Eichinger, R. W. (1989). *Preventing derailment: What to do before it's too late.* Greensboro, NC: Center for Creative Leadership.

McCauley, C. D., & Martineau, J. W. (1998). *Reaching your development goals.* Greensboro, NC: Center for Creative Leadership.

Ordering Information

TO GET MORE INFORMATION, TO ORDER OTHER IDEAS INTO ACTION GUIDEBOOKS, OR TO FIND OUT ABOUT BULK-ORDER DISCOUNTS, PLEASE CONTACT US BY PHONE AT 336-545-2810 OR VISIT OUR ONLINE BOOKSTORE AT WWW.CCL.ORG/GUIDEBOOKS.